When Someone Dies

When Someone Dies

Sharon Greenlee
Illustrations by Bill Drath

PEACHTREE PUBLISHERS
Atlanta

Published by
PEACHTREE PUBLISHERS, LTD.
494 Armour Circle, NE
Atlanta, Georgia 30324

Text and Illustrations © 1992 Sharon Greenlee

Design by Candace J. Magee

Fifth printing (1998)

Library of Congress Cataloging-in-Publication Data

Greenlee, Sharon, 1935-
      When someone dies / Sharon Greenlee ; illustrations by Bill Drath..
        p. cm.
      ISBN 1-56145-044-8
      1. Grief—Juvenile literature. 2. Bereavement—Psychological
  aspects—Juvenile literature. 3. Death—Psychological aspects—
  Juvenile literature. [1. Death. 2. Grief.] I. Drath, Bill, ill. II. Title.
  BF575.G7G69 1992
  155.9'37—dc20   92-10250
                                                              CIP
  Printed in China   AC

For Anna and Andrew
and
Kim, Julie and Kathy
and in memory of
Dave

Also in memory of
Dennis

and
Bill Drath

When someone dies,
you can't talk together on the phone anymore,
but you can still remember
what the two of you used to say.

It's like you're away from each other on a long vacation,
and you have to keep remembering that this time,
one of you can't come back.

When someone you love a lot dies,
you get sad, empty feelings.

You don't even know why you're feeling so bad . . .

until you remember all over again.

Sometimes you feel mad inside . . .
mad that you're alone, unable to see that special face,
hear the voice, or share thoughts, feelings
and times together.

People don't go away like this on purpose,
or even set out to make you sad.
That's just what happens . . . when someone dies.

If the person who died was very important to you,
you get to worrying that all the other important people
might leave too.

I've never heard of it happening that way,
but it's hard not to think about it.

When people die, they can't come to your house anymore.
You wonder what they'd look like now,
and you do all you can to make a picture of them
in your mind.

If it was a very special person who died, you don't
get a birthday present from that person anymore . . .
not even a card.

Oftentimes you go to sleep at night and dream about
the person still being with you. You feel so happy.
Then you wake up and the dream isn't true, and the sad
feels almost bigger than it felt in the beginning.

It will usually start to get better again . . . about lunchtime.

After someone dies,
lots of people hang around together;
people coming and going, crying—even laughing.
It can be confusing, especially if you're a kid.

It seems grownups
don't think about talking to you,
or maybe they just don't know what to say.
Nothing in life seems like it used to be.
At times like this, nothing in life IS like it used to be.

Even if you're all grown up,
you still don't always understand,
or know what to do or say to help yourself,
or someone else.

So, whether you're a kid or a tall person,
there are a few things you can do, when someone dies,
that might help a little bit.

Find the person you love and trust the most
and GO AHEAD AND CRY.
You will feel better afterward, even if you cry so hard
your nose plugs up and it's hard to get your breath.

Don't worry if the other person cries too.

Something good happens when
you cry together with someone you love.
You'll both feel better,
even if it doesn't seem like it at the time.

Sometimes it helps to write a letter
to the person who died. Share your special feelings.
Remember the fun or silly times you had together—
laugh with the memories; cry if you need to.

And if you want to say you're sorry for something you didn't
get to say in person, say it in your letter.

Even if you can't
write it all down
by yourself,
ask someone you trust to write as you tell about it.
A teacher or counselor might be just the person to help you.

Remember, we just have to go through those
times of feeling bad, when someone dies,
and so do the people around us.

But when we take time to think our thoughts and
listen to our feelings, parts of each day seem to get better.
Even though there will be times when we'll need to cry
all over again.

It's the hardest of times.
Yet, it seems easier when we hold tight
to the happy memories.

When we talk about those memories and smile
thinking of times we had with each other,
it's almost like keeping a special part of the person
RIGHT BESIDE US   in our hearts.

And when this happens,
a beautiful secret of life reveals itself—

All those experiences we shared lovingly on earth
are gracefully woven, over time,
into a wonderful cape of comfort that fits all who loved
the one who went away.

Sharon Greenlee

Author Biography

Sharon Greenlee, a former elementary-school teacher, holds a master's degree in Elementary Education from Drake University and teaches courses in counseling at the University of Wyoming. She focuses primarily on counseling grieving children through writing therapy. She lives in Centennial, Wyoming, with her husband Richard, an elementary-school principal.

Illustrator Biography

Bill Drath was born in 1915 in Wisconsin. A graduate of the University of Wisconsin, he served in the Army during World War II (earning a Bronze Star) and the Korean War, retiring in 1966 as a lieutenant colonel. Drath also illustrated IF I FOUND A WISTFUL UNI-CORN and SOUTHERN IS. . . . He died in 1991.